HOW TO NAVIGATE
THE ELECTION PROCESS
AND
SELECT YOUR CANDIDATES

MARY MEEKS

PAGE PUBLISHING, INC.
New York, NY

First originally published by Page Publishing, Inc. 2018

ISBN 978-1-64214-382-9 (Paperback)
ISBN 978-1-64214-383-6 (Digital)

Printed in the United States of America

Acknowledgements

Thank you, Angie, for prompting me to write this book, and for your feedback along the way.

Thank you, Julia, for providing content suggestions and writing the summary.

Thank you, Charlotte, for your encouragement and telling me I 'should write books.'

Thank you, Dad, for teaching me to consider perspectives beyond my own as I form opinions, and expecting me to be my best through life's twists and turns.

Introduction

THE MORE PEOPLE who thoughtfully engage in our election process the more representative our government will be. To that end, the purpose of this book is to equip people with strategies to determine which political candidate to vote for *without* being swept up in the drama that, sadly, is prevalent in our election cycles. Begin to notice when your feelings are manipulated. Doing so will empower you to navigate election season well.

Our system of government is designed for and depends on citizens' participation. Unlike many countries, we do not have royalty or a designated *ruling class* that is above the law. We have the unique opportunity to select from our peers who will represent us. If they do not keep their word, we have the power to remove them from office by replacing them with someone else in the next election. We need not be victims of corrupt leadership. A peaceful, orderly transfer of power is our heritage. By educating yourself and voting, you become part of the solution.

CHAPTER 1

Voter Registration

FIND OUT WHEN elections are held in your area, then mark your calendar. Some years there are two elections, some years there may be none. Typically, there are deadlines before which you must register to vote in order to participate in an election. Ask your state's Board of Elections what they are in your area and plan accordingly. If you miss the deadline, register anyway so you can participate in the next election. It might be sooner than you think!

If you are already registered to vote, confirm the Board of Elections has your current information including your name and address.

Voter registration is handled by your state of residence, likely by their *Board of Elections*. To start, do a web search with *voter registration,* plus the name of your state. Some states assist in voter registration by offering the service through the Department of Motor Vehicles when you initially register your vehicle. You may be required to select a political party. While there are several, the most common are: Democratic, Libertarian, and Republican. You could conduct an internet search to learn your options. If you are new to the process or simply do not *fit* into any given political party's way of thinking, selecting *Independent* may be appropriate for you if that is an option in your state.

If you have difficulty finding the information online, ask a reference librarian at the local public library to assist. You could also ask a trusted friend to help.

CHAPTER 2

Sample Ballot

YOUR SAMPLE BALLOT is your *GPS* of sorts. It is a key component to getting you through election season while maintaining your sanity.

It is a preview of your ballot. To learn when it will be available and how you can access it, conduct an internet search with *sample ballot vote (your state)*. Once you have arrived at the site, you will be asked to enter information such as your name. This ensures you will view *your* ballot, and not your neighbor's which may be different depending on how boundaries are drawn. Then download and print a copy to use as a research guide. It lists all offices, candidates, and local issues you will see on your actual ballot. If you are not registered to vote, you may not have access to a sample ballot.

Such ballots are only available for a designated length of time prior to any election. You may get this information directly from your state's Board of Elections. When you see the first yard sign or hear the first political radio ad, you will know it is time to obtain your sample ballot and begin your research.

Your ballot may include candidates for federal, state, and local offices, in addition to state or local ballot initiatives. Some political offices allow candidates to mention which party they affiliate (partisan), other offices, such as judicial seats, do not (nonpartisan). Federal offices include president, US senator, and US representative. State offices include governor, state senator, state representative, clerk of superior court, district court judge, and district attorney. Local offices include mayor, county commissioner, sheriff, and board of education. Referendums and ballot measures may also appear on your ballot.

If this is overwhelming, pause. Simply choose one candidate or one issue to research and begin. (Instructions are found in the next chapter.) Continue researching when you are ready. On election day, bring your completed sample ballot with you to the voting booth. No need to memorize your selections!

On election day, your ballot may offer *straight party voting* as an option. That means if you select one party, the vote counting machine will automatically vote for all candidates in that party up for election. For example, if you select straight-party Republican, it will select all Republicans on the ballot and vote for them. If you select straight-party Democrat, it will select all Democrats on the ballot and vote for them. I urge you not to take this option as it has become common for politicians to masquerade as something they are not, only to show their true colors *after* elections. You are an individual with the capacity for thought, thus, let *your* thoughts be heard by voting for each candidate you researched one at a time. Note that nonpartisan offices and local issues are not included when one selects the *straight party* option.

After election night, stay engaged. You may need to vote again in a runoff election. Once election results are settled and their term begins, contact your elected official periodically with your perspective on specific issues.[1] How can they know what you want if they do not hear from you? Communicating with them will help them represent you.

---

[1]   Elected officials' contact information will be found on their government website. Conduct an internet search including their last name, office, state, and *gov.* Their official government site will offer a variety of ways to contact them by physical mail, phone, etc.

CHAPTER 3

How to Research a Candidate

THE PROCESS of researching a candidate has multiple layers and is a bit like peeling back the layers of an onion. First locate a source of information, gather data on issues and endorsements, examine them, then notate any gaps in information (what was left out or glossed over). Consider the tone in which information is conveyed, the behavior of each candidate, and the behavior of those who endorse them. This research process will require you to think, ask, and decide.

Use primary and secondary sources to uncover information. A primary source will be the candidate themselves, or what they say about themselves in advertisements or on their website. If it is feasible, meet the candidate and listen to what they say about their policies. Ask questions. Secondary sources will be websites, news articles, radio, and other advertising by those who endorse the candidate. Keep in mind, some people speak the truth and others deceive. This is one reason it is important to dig a bit for information and to inspect their endorsements to capture an accurate picture of who your candidates are.

To locate a candidate's website, enter key words in your internet search such as their last name, the office they hope to win, the year, your state, the district number, and anything else that would identify the candidate. For example, if there is a candidate by the name of McIntosh who wants to be a representative for California's 3rd district in 2020, you may enter *McIntosh for representative district 3 California 2020* in the search bar. (To my knowledge, no candidate by the name of McIntosh is running for the aforementioned office. The name was randomly chosen to offer an example of how to enter keywords in a search.) The web address may be mentioned in advertising so you may not have to search for it at all. I would not recommend using *wiki* type sites in this search as they can be edited by anyone at any time which leaves the candidate vulnerable to being misrepresented.

Once you have found the website, locate the list of issues. At this point, begin collecting data. Use a new page to document what you find for each political office and build a chart so you can view each candidate's information side by side. This will reduce the likelihood you will be swept away in the drama of any given moment. Organize your charts in a notebook or just staple them together.

To build a chart, make at least three columns: one for the issues and one for each of the candidates' names. Next, make as many rows as there are issues on the website. Once you have noted where candidates stand on issues, list who endorses them. Here is a sample chart based on two make-believe candidates for US House of Representatives:

Issue	Candidate A	Candidate B
Border Security	US Border laws are to be enforced. They protect our citizens.	We are citizens of the world. No need for borders. Anyone from anywhere should be able to come and go as they please.
Second Amendment	These rights should be taken away.	These rights should be protected.
Abortions	Abortions should not be funded by taxpayer money.	Abortions should continue to be funded by taxpayer money.
Corporate Tax Rate	No information found	Rate should be competitive with other developed nations.
Endorsements	Governor C, Sheriff D, organization E	Senator A, Firefighter R, organization J.

For some races, just making a chart will provide enough data for you to determine who you will support. For other races, you may need to dig a bit more to distinguish a difference between the candidates.

Consider the depth of the information offered on each issue. When the candidate listed their views, were they specific or vague? How much information was offered? If there was very little information, ask yourself why. Why might a candidate not reveal their thoughts on the issues? If they have no thoughts, would you want them to represent you?

Some candidates have clearly defined goals for the future and communicate clear, common sense steps to reach them. Sometimes necessary steps toward a goal are not as pleasant as we would like them to be. For example, it may be necessary for you to exercise if you want to be lean and fit. If being lean and fit is important to you, you will likely decide to go through the rigors of exercising consistently over time to achieve the desired result. It is up to you to scrutinize candidates' ideas to determine whom you will support.

Other candidates are vague and hope for *blue skies and green lights for all*. While such may leave us feeling good for the moment, it is crucial to remain focused on your fact-gathering mission. Perhaps, make a side note in your chart for that candidate such as *warm and fuzzy* or *lacks specifics*. Be real. Having only blue skies means there is no rain, which means crops would die, leading to famine. Having only green lights always means nobody has red lights, which would lead to traffic jams, which means you might miss your afternoon appointment. As you consider the candidates, determine what they want to accomplish. What are their stated goals? Do they have constructive ideas of their own or is their main message one of resistance?

If there is missing information or a candidate does not address an issue, ponder *why not?* On the chart with make-believe candidates, Candidate A did not offer any information about the corporate tax rate. Do they not have an opinion about it? Why else might a candidate not provide their views? What about the folks who endorse Candidate A? What do they think about the corporate tax rate? If Candidate A truly has no opinion about it, then they have no understanding of its implications. Would you grant decision-making power to someone who is ignorant on such an important issue? Voting for someone gives them such power.

Also, consider the tone in which information is presented. Does your information source highlight drama (whether real or invented), or does it skip the gossip and go straight for candidates' views on any given issue? Begin to notice word usage and whether it stirs emotions or summons reason. For instance, consider the phrase *political enemy*. Why might someone use *enemy* when referring to a person running for a political office? What purpose would it serve? In sports, teams with historic rivalries are referred to as *rivals* or *opponents*. So, why *political enemy?* Who would benefit from such wording?

Words can have multiple meanings, so pay attention to what is being said. Two candidates with opposite views about public education may both say "Education is my top priority." Excellent. Find out what they mean. What specific problem have they identified with education that they have made it their top priority? What specific steps will they take to improve education? Is their goal to empower local classroom teachers to make professional judgments about curricula or is their goal to empower the federal government to make such decisions for all students nationwide? Uncover the meaning behind the words used. Listen carefully. Notice context.

When researching judges, you may come across the term *nonpartisan* and the phrase *not legislate from the bench*. Nonpartisan means without reference to a political party with the purpose of remaining impartial (fair); not favoring one side over another.[2]* Elections for judges are considered nonpartisan. To *legislate from the bench* is an overreach of power by a judge. Only the legislative branch (senators and representatives) have the authority to create laws (to legislate).[3] Thus, if a judge states they *will not legislate from the bench*, it suggests they respect the authority of the Constitution and simply interpret the law.

---

[2]   https://www.floridabar.org/wp-content/uploads/2017/04/voterinfobrochure-2016-ada.pdf.

[3]   https://www.docsoffreedom.org/readings/separation-of-powers-with-checks-and-balances

Take care as you gather data for your chart. Consider this illustration: a licensed medical care provider definitively states that the way for people to regain their health is to eat vegetables. Some people will agree, and some people will disagree. Some people will want to discredit this perspective simply because it differs from their own. The anti-vegetable crowd might make false statements about the medical professional's personal life or construe stories that make the casual observer wonder whether his license was ever valid in the first place—stories that have nothing at all to do with the merit of his perspective on health and vegetables.

In politics, a candidate may offer logical and simple solutions that are not popular. Look and listen carefully for the content of the candidate's message. Listening to what someone *else* says about it leaves you vulnerable to *that* person's opinion mixed in with the candidate's message. If you only listen to the aforementioned anti-vegetable crowd, you may conclude the medical professional is rude, unfit to advise, and uncaring. However, if you gather information from the primary source, you might agree on the issue. On the other hand, you may disagree. Okay, so disagree. Don't eat your vegetables. It is a free country! Just go on about your nonvegetarian way being kind and decent to those who think eating vegetables is a good idea. People can disagree on a topic and still be civil toward one another. There is no excuse for personal attacks on a candidate, verbal or otherwise. Remember, this process is about you uncovering facts. Do your best to get firsthand information and think for yourself.

Consider what character traits would you like your elected official to have. Which candidate embodies them? What about their endorsements? Do you excuse and tolerate name-calling, gossip, slander, isolation, threats, blackmail, and other types of bullying? Or do you expect your elected officials to rise above this? Keep in mind, we are all human, and as such, have been less than ideal at times. Therefore, consider the sum of a candidate's beliefs, actions, words, and associations. Take care not to decide the fate of a candidate based on one sound bite that may have been taken out of context. Look at the whole picture.

If you discuss candidates with coworkers or friends, ask them why or why not they support a candidate. If the answer is something like "Oh, he has such great hair! Of course, I will vote for him!" you will know how seriously to take that person's opinion.

It is possible for a candidate to genuinely care, have pure intentions, *and* be misguided. Learn where they stand on issues and decide whether that makes any sense to you before pledging your support. Do not vote for a School Board candidate just because they smiled at you at the local market. Of course, they smiled. They want your vote! It might turn out you'll change your mind as you uncover more information in the research process.

As you consider secondary sources of information, find out who supports the candidate. With whom do they associate? Who endorses them? Where do these people (or groups) stand on issues? Are they peaceful or do they have a history of violence? Do they exemplify civility or do they stir dissent and rebellion? Do they promote peace or are they silent when there is violence? Do they respect due process and the law or make efforts to circumvent it? There are countless groups who spout opinions about various candidates. Start to notice who pays for the advertising. Ask yourself questions such as: do they value the same things I do? If they are saying anything negative about their opponent, are they simply stating the views or voting record to highlight the differences between them? Do they spend the bulk of their advertising building up the candidate they support or tearing down the opponent?

Using these strategies will help you determine which candidate most closely matches what you believe. You are a unique individual with your own life experiences; thus, it is unlikely any candidate will believe the same way you do on every topic. In some cases, it may be a matter of selecting which candidate would more closely align with your ideals. It may turn out you cannot support either candidate with a clear conscience. Spend some time contemplating why you have reached that conclusion and do as you see best. However, do not use that as an excuse not to participate in the election process at all. Continue on to the next line item on your sample ballot, make a chart, gather information, and so on.

On election day, once you have obtained your ballot and reached the voting booth, you are not obligated to vote for every race and every issue. If you have not learned enough about a candidate to make an informed decision, consider not voting for that particular office. Just skip that option and move on to the next choice. You are not required to vote for every issue or office. Consider the alternative: let's say you voted for someone but don't know what they believe. What if it turns out they believe the opposite of what you believe? What if they win?

CHAPTER 4

A Note on Advertising

MOST EFFECTIVE ADVERTISING for any product or service draws upon our emotions to connect the product or service with how our lives will be better when we experience it. For example, they promise we will look younger, have more energy, feel healthy, be more attractive, be more popular, etc. if we use their product or service. Feelings are stirred by the use of music, images, and words. The greater your awareness the quicker you can determine what they are trying to sell you. When politicians are campaigning before an election, they are *selling* their services. They advertise to obtain your support. As with advertising for any other product or service, you want to research a bit before you *buy* it.

Advertising is not inherently good or evil. Simply being aware of its elements will reduce the chances you'll be swept away in the drama of the presentation. Also note, the candidate with the best idea may not have the money or the resources to produce fancy advertising.

Here are some tools:

- Music: if it is dark and scary, it may stir feelings of anxiety. If it is lighthearted or upbeat, it may instill hope.
- Color: if it is black and white, it may harken to your grandparents' days when *all was well* or it may be used to

depict a scene of good people down on their luck. Colors may be bold, harsh, or calming.

- Light: if there is little light, it may suggest hopelessness. If it is bright, it may suggest better times ahead.
- Images: pictures of children, firefighters, teachers, Olympians, police officers, the elderly, a bustling city, trash-filled alleys, well-manicured parks.
- Words: specific, vague, promises, warnings, words of comfort.

For what purpose are these elements being used? Is it a picture of a brighter tomorrow if you vote for that candidate? What will be brighter? How will that happen? Are specific steps delineated or is it an empty, feel-good message? Who doesn't want to feel good? Skilled politicians know this. If an ad says "a number of sources say," ask yourself questions like:

- What is the number one, three, seventeen?
- Who was that source? Did they disclose their identity? If they did not disclose the name of the source, do you still trust it? Might the source have been the person in line with them at the fast food place? Maybe it was voices in their head (multiple voices which would make it more than one)?

Also consider who paid for the message. Does the candidate approve?

Political ads tend to focus on the future and how we feel about it. Do we feel uncertain? Hopeful? Fearful? Full of anticipation? One goal in such advertising is to connect positive feelings about the future to a specific candidate. Sometimes a single ad will also attempt to connect negative feelings about the future to that candidate's opponent. Take note and be aware of the tactics used so you can remain clear-minded enough to think for yourself. One candidate may actually believe their opponent intends, metaphorically speaking, to *throw Granny off a cliff.* With the strategies offered in this book, you can determine for yourself whether you believe it is truth or slander.

In summary, notice the delivery of the message, as well as the message itself.

Beware of the manipulation of your feelings. This may be the very thing that overwhelms many during election season.

CHAPTER 5

Smoke Screens

IN THEATER, smoke screens are used to distract the audience from what is really happening on stage. For example, perhaps there is a quick set change that if seen would take away from the element of surprise intended in the production. Some form of smoke is produced to provide cover for the transition. Smoke screens in theater are neither good nor bad. They simply serve a purpose.

Let's examine how smoke screens might be used in political campaigns. If, for whatever reason, people who oppose a candidate want to suppress their message, they might choose to verbally attack the candidate about unrelated issues. The attacks might be partial truths taken out of context or they may be complete fabrications. The accusations might be lies about their personal lives, their professional lives, or their family. The purpose of the attacks might be to get the general population in the habit of questioning everything the candidate says or does, reducing the chances that candidate's ideas will be seriously considered. In order to have this level of impact, they might need to be persistent in their attacks over a period of time. If you sense this may be happening, take a step back and pay attention to whether the accusers critique all candidates with the same intensity or whether they are heavy-handed with only one candidate. What might that reveal about the accusers?

Character assassination is a technique used to discredit a person over a period of time, criticizing, questioning, and doubting everything about them. There may be orchestrated efforts to destroy someone's reputation to the point of public mistrust or disgust. Such actions can serve as a smoke screen to distract from the content of a political candidate's message. Ask yourself why anyone would choose to destroy someone else's reputation. Who would benefit from such behavior? Do they offer any solutions of their own? Why distract the general population from learning all they can about a candidate's policies? Why not have an open, honest discussions about ideas? Keep in mind that stating facts about a person's voting record or quoting what they have said in context is not necessarily mudslinging. At some point, it is necessary to distinguish oneself from one's opponent in order to gain supporters.

Notice what your information sources focus on: Is it to educate and inform, or is it to stir emotions? Search for sources that provide facts served without mudslinging.

CHAPTER 6

Primary Elections

PRIMARY ELECTIONS DETERMINE the top candidate from each party whose names then appear on the ballots for the general election.

Specific rules for *primary elections* vary from state to state, but the following comparison to sports parallels the primary process in many states. Consider two political groups: purple and gray.

In sports tournaments, there are play-off games, then a championship game. Think of primary elections as the tournament games that determine who plays in the final competition. The purple group must select its top candidate, and the gray group must select its top candidate. The general election is the equivalent of a *championship* event in sports. The top purple candidate will run against the top gray candidate. The one who wins a general election fills that political office for a designated period of time.

All people, regardless of whether they are purple or gray (or any other affiliation), show up at the polling places on election day to determine which candidate will represent them. The one who earns the most votes wins the election for that position in government (county commissioner, senator, sheriff, judge, labor secretary, or such). The exception is for the office of president of the United States who is determined by the electoral college.

Elections differ from sports in this way: if you are from the purple community, *you are not obligated to vote for the purple candidate.* After learning about both candidates, you might determine that one particular gray candidate would better represent you this time around. This does not make you a traitor. It may simply mean you are thinking for yourself and determining what makes the most sense to you based on your research. This is freedom. You get to decide. Furthermore, you are under no obligation to tell anyone for whom you voted.

Into the weeds

- A few locations hold what is called a *jungle primary* in which the top two vote-earners from any given party make it to the general election, regardless of their party affiliation. In this case, two purple candidates may go against one another during the general election.
- In some states, you may only participate in the primary election of your chosen party.
- In other states, if you have selected *Independent* as your party (meaning, you are not affiliated with a political party), you may choose which party's primary you would like to participate in (for example, if your beliefs are more in line with the Democratic Party than the Republican Party, you may opt to vote for the list of Democrats running for the various offices).

Ask your state's Board of Elections when the primary and general elections are held in your area. Mark your calendar. Not every government position is voted on every year. The frequency of elections for any given office is determined by the length of time each office is held. For example, each U.S. representative in the House serves a two-year term. Toward the end of that term, an election is held to determine whether or by whom they will be replaced. U.S. Senators each serve a six-year term; thus, every six years an election is held to determine whether or by whom they will be replaced. There are one hundred senate seats. Each of our fifty states is represented by two senators. Originally, U.S. senators were appointed by the legislative body from the state they represented. But now, they are voted upon by the general population within each state. Elections for the

US Senate are held on a rotating basis, such that about one-third of the senate seats are up for election every two years.

If any part of the election process does not make sense to you, ask. Ask a local librarian where or how to find the answers. Ask the people working at the Board of Elections (or whatever your state has named the people in charge of elections in your state). Get answers to your questions. Your vote matters.

CHAPTER 7

Definitions and Other Resources

GENERAL ELECTIONS are the typically the final election in the process and determine who will serve in that particular office.
Special elections might be held when politicians step out of office before their term ends and need to be replaced. In some localities, their replacement is appointed. In others, a special election is held to determine their replacement.

Runoff elections are held when no single candidate has earned enough votes to win the general election (*enough votes* is determined by local laws). Typically, the top two vote-earners will be on the ballot for this type of special election. Voters would have to return to their polling places to determine the winner.

Presidential elections are general elections held in early November of every fourth year for the office of President of the United States.

Midterm elections are general elections held halfway through a President's four-year term in office.

Gubernatorial elections are held every four years, with the exception of Vermont and New Hampshire where they are held every two years. (*Gubernatorial* means it is for the office of governor of a state.) Not all states hold such elections the same year. About ten of our fifty states hold them the same year as presidential elections. Most others hold them two years after presidential elections and the remaining states, including New Jersey, Mississippi, and Kentucky, hold them in the odd-numbered years between.[4] Whether your state holds them in any given year will be reflected on your sample ballot.

Primary elections determine the top candidate from each party whose names then appear on the ballots for the general election.

County Commissioner determines how taxpayers' money is (or is not) spent locally.

Sheriff upholds and enforces the law.

Board of Education determines policies impacting every family in your school district.

Precinct is the area or neighborhood in which you live and therefore vote.

Rep can be an abbreviation for either *Republican* or *Representative*. Look for context clues. For example, Rep. John Doe would likely mean Representative John Doe. Just as Sen. John Doe would mean Senator John Doe.

Websites to use as a resource:

- Senate.gov offers a wealth of information including the election years for each of your two US Senators, how to contact them, and information on current legislation.
- House.gov offers similar information for the US House of Representatives.

---

[4] State Yellow Book, Spring 2017, Volume 29, Number 1, page x. Leadership Directories, Inc., www.leadershipdirectories.com 1407 Broadway, Ste 318, NY NY 10018 212-627-4140p 212-645-0931f.

Civil servant is a term used to describe the role of an elected official in the United States as their purpose is to do the will of the people they represent. Our form of government is a Democratic Republic. We determine who represents us (that is the Democratic part), then they are to do what we tell them to as our representatives (that is the Republic part).

Constituents are the people represented by the elected official. For example, the constituents of a governor are the citizens who reside in their state.

Congress is another name for the legislative branch which includes the Senate and the House of Representatives, which is often just called *the House.*

Legislator is an elected official in congress, a senator, or representative who creates laws

Electoral College is the process used to select the next President. The number of votes each state is granted is this: one for each Senator, one for each Representative. Delegates are chosen (by different means in different states) and the delegates vote. In some states, the presidential candidate who wins the popular vote is granted all of the electoral votes in a *winner takes all* scenario. In other states, the delegates' votes are proportional to the popular vote. For example, if a presidential candidate wins one-third of the popular vote, they will get one-third of the electoral votes; the other candidate who won two-thirds of the popular vote would get two-thirds of the electoral votes. Rules for delegates vary from state to state. Electors may not hold a federal office. The candidate who earns 270 such votes becomes the next president.[5]

---

[5]   State Yellow Book, Spring 2017, Volume 29, Number 1, page 1310. Leadership Directories, Inc., www.leadershipdirectories.com 1407 Broadway, Ste 318, NY NY 10018 212-627-4140p 212-645-0931f.

CHAPTER 8

Navigating the Nonsense

HERE ARE SOME suggestions to guide you through the times when you are overwhelmed and want to throw up your hands and quit.

Don't listen to or look at political ads for a little while. Just go to the direct sources for information, such as the candidate's website. Be wary of information you might have read on a *wiki* type of site in which anyone anywhere can change the information to say whatever they wish, whether true or false.

When you are tempted to quit, what led up to that? What were you listening to or reading just before you felt that way? Were you overcome with dread because you were awakened to the gravity of a situation? Were you bombarded with anger and hatred in an ad discrediting a candidate? Or is there some other reason?

If talking with friends on or off of social media stresses you out, stop discussing politics with them for a while so you can think clearly. Consider *what* is being said, and *how* it is being said. What about it bothers you? Are they policy discussions or are they personal attacks without merit against the candidate? Is the goal of the communication to belittle an opponent or to point out policy differences with that opponent in a civil manner? Review the chapter on candidate research to gain clarity. Many accusations will fly. Stay clear-minded. Make educated decisions.

If this still feels like too much, pause. Take a deep breath, then pick one issue that is important to you. Learn where each candidate stands on that one issue. After you have completed research comparing candidates on one issue, you may be energized to investigate a second issue. You can do this. It is better to do some research than none at all.

When people make the effort to educate themselves and participate in our election process, our government will more clearly reflect who we are. We are a diverse people with a myriad of perspectives and life experiences. As more of us participate the more balanced our representation will be. This balance will ensure our rights are protected, not just the interests of a select few who are well-funded and well-connected. We have the privilege of selecting our own leadership. Why not elect the very best?

Tools for Success

Election Process Navigation Checklist:

- ☐ I have registered to vote.
- ☐ I have verified the address of my polling location, it is _____________________.
- ☐ I know the date of the election. It is ____ (day) ___________ (month).
- ☐ I know the polling hours on election day. They begin at _____ a.m. and end at ______p.m.
- ☐ I have notated election day on my calendar.
- ☐ I have printed my sample ballot.
- ☐ I have researched candidates.
- ☐ I have researched local issues.
- ☐ I have filled out my sample ballot. It is ready to bring with me to the voting booth on election day.

Candidate Research Template

Issues	Candidate A	Candidate B

Local Issue Research Template

Local Issue	Arguments *for*	Arguments *against*

www.ingramcontent.com/pod-product-compliance
Lightning Source LLC
Chambersburg PA
CBHW051239250726
48656CB00003B/1024